FINGERPICKING
ITALIAN SONGS

ISBN: 978-1-4950-6317-6

Visit Hal Leonard Online at
www.halleonard.com

Contact Us:
Hal Leonard
7777 West Bluemound Road
Milwaukee, WI 53213
Email: info@halleonard.com

In Europe contact:
Hal Leonard Europe Limited
Distribution Centre, Newmarket Road
Bury St Edmunds, Suffolk, IP33 3YB
Email: info@halleonardeurope.com

In Australia contact:
Hal Leonard Australia Pty. Ltd.
4 Lentara Court
Cheltenham, Victoria, 3192 Australia
Email: info@halleonard.com.au

FINGERPICKING
ITALIAN SONGS

INTRODUCTION TO FINGERSTYLE GUITAR

Fingerstyle (a.k.a. fingerpicking) is a guitar technique that means you literally pick the strings with your right-hand fingers and thumb. This contrasts with the conventional technique of strumming and playing single notes with a pick (a.k.a. flatpicking). For fingerpicking, you can use any type of guitar: acoustic steel-string, nylon-string classical, or electric.

THE RIGHT HAND

The most common right-hand position is shown here.

Use a high wrist; arch your palm as if you were holding a ping-pong ball. Keep the thumb outside and away from the fingers, and let the fingers do the work rather than lifting your whole hand.

The thumb generally plucks the bottom strings with downstrokes on the left side of the thumb and thumbnail. The other fingers pluck the higher strings using upstrokes with the fleshy tip of the fingers and fingernails. The thumb and fingers should pluck one string per stroke and not brush over several strings.

Another picking option you may choose to use is called hybrid picking (a.k.a. plectrum-style fingerpicking). Here, the pick is usually held between the thumb and first finger, and the three remaining fingers are assigned to pluck the higher strings.

THE LEFT HAND

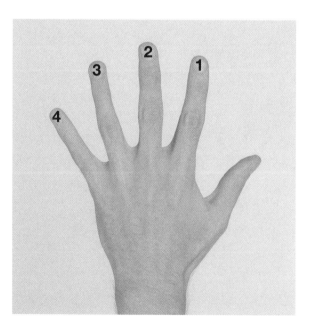

The left-hand fingers are numbered 1 through 4.

Be sure to keep your fingers arched, with each joint bent; if they flatten out across the strings, they will deaden the sound when you fingerpick. As a general rule, let the strings ring as long as possible when playing fingerstyle.

Anema e core
(With All My Heart)

English Lyric by Mann Curtis and Harry Akst
Italian Lyric by Tito Manlio
Music by Salve d'Esposito

Intro
Moderately slow

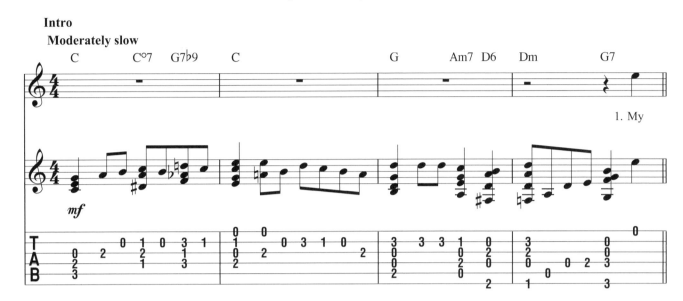

1. My

§ Verse

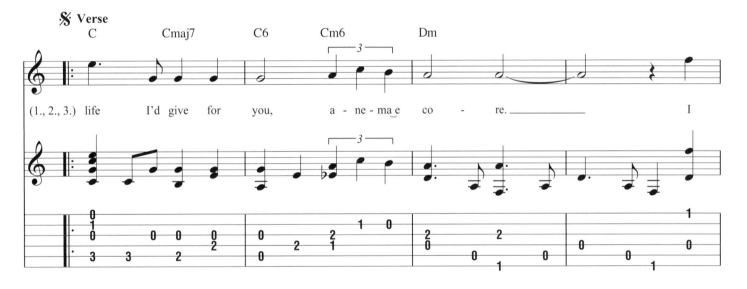

(1., 2., 3.) life I'd give for you, a - ne - ma e co - re. _____ I

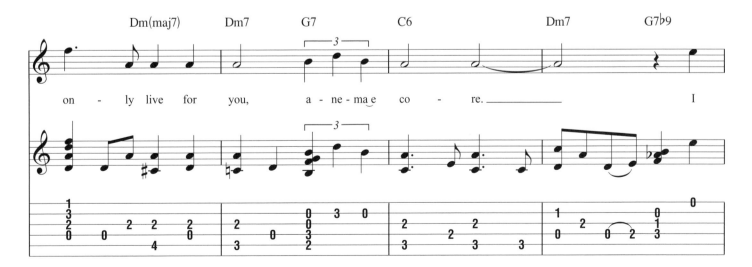

on - ly live for you, a - ne - ma e co - re. _____ I

have but one de - sire and it's to love you _____ with all my

heart, with all my soul, my whole life through. _____ From

stars I'll make your crown and kneel be - fore you. _____ I

pray you'll take my hand, for I a - dore you.

O - pen up the doors lead - ing to heav - en, _____

_____ a heav - en mine and yours, a - ne - ma e

To Coda ⊕

7

co - re. _____   2. My   co - re. _____

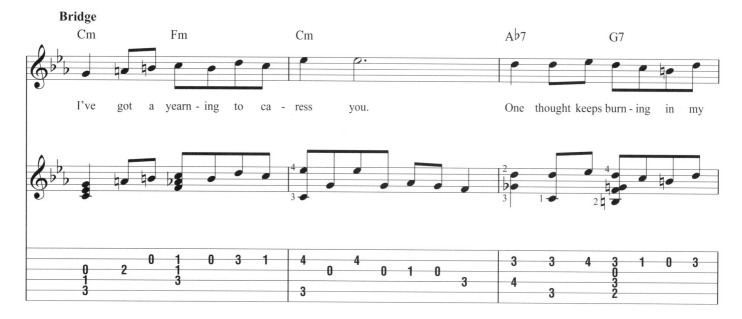

Bridge

I've   got   a   yearn - ing   to   ca - ress   you.   One   thought keeps burn - ing   in   my

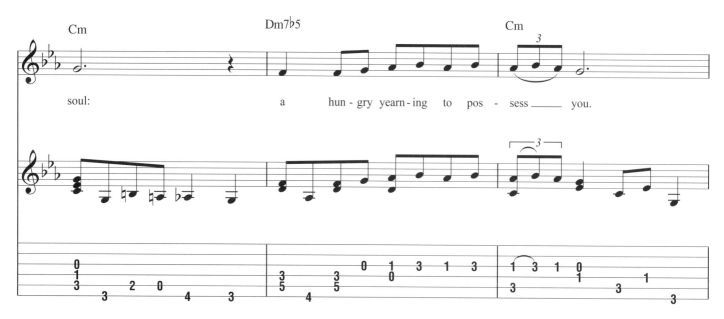

soul: a   hun - gry yearn - ing   to   pos - sess ____ you.

It's far be - yond con - trol.   I   want your love for now, for -

D.S. al Coda
(no repeat)

ev - er.   I   want your heart   and   soul.   3. My

Coda

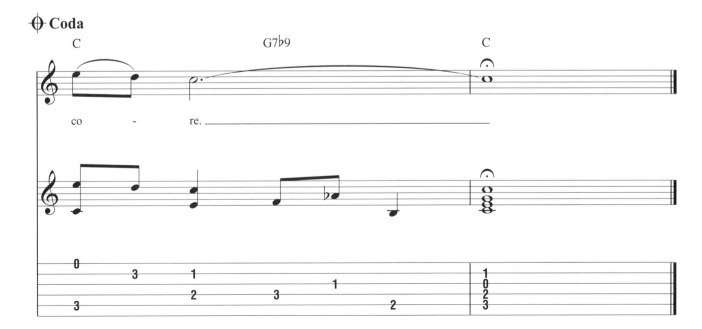

co -   re. _____

Arrivederci Roma
(Goodbye to Rome)
from the Motion Picture SEVEN HILLS OF ROME

Words and Music by Carl Sigman, Ranucci Renato, Sandro Giovanni and Peidro Garinei

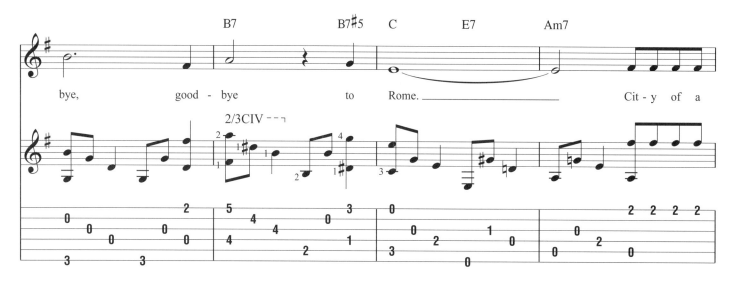

mil - lion moon - lit plac - es, cit - y of a mil - lion warm em -

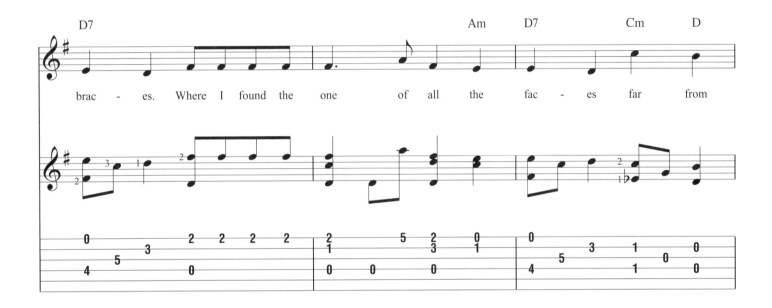

brac - es. Where I found the one of all the fac - es far from

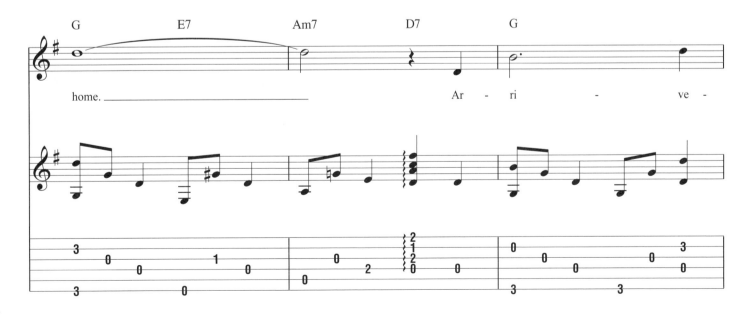

home. _____ Ar - ri - ve -

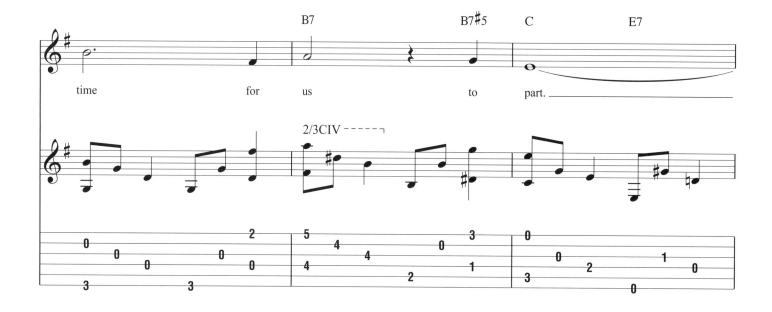

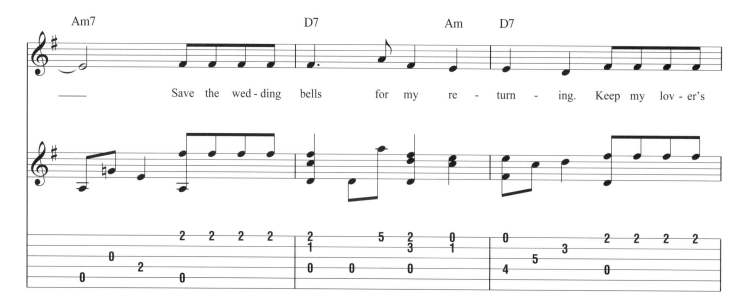

arms out-stretched and yearn - ing. Please be sure the flame of love keeps

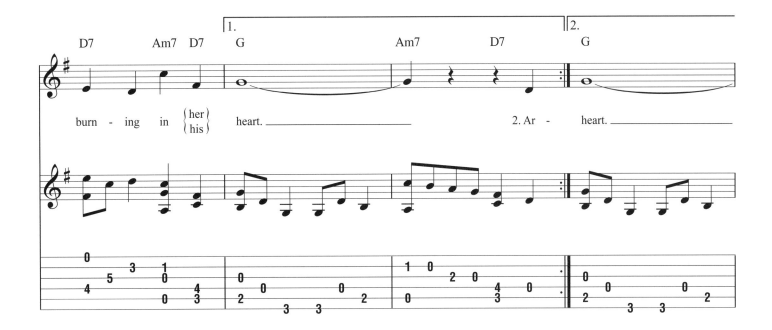

burn - ing in {her}{his} heart. _____ 2. Ar - heart. _____

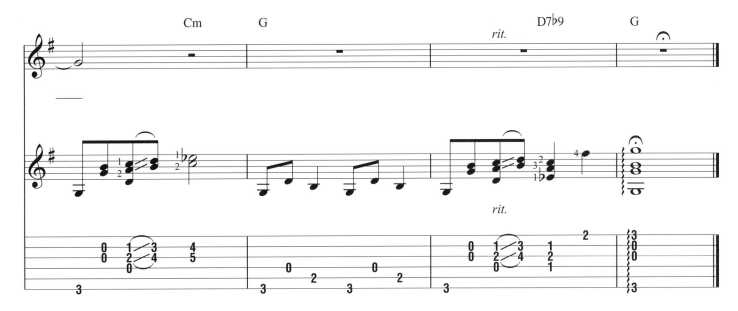

Cinema Paradiso

from CINEMA PARADISO

By Ennio Morricone and Andrea Morricone

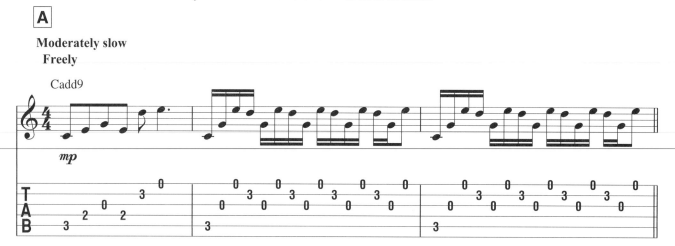

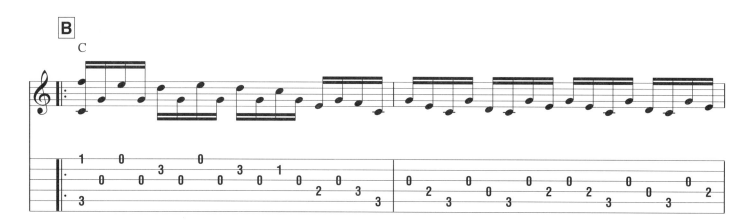

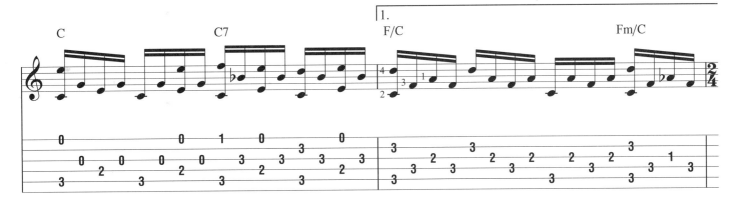

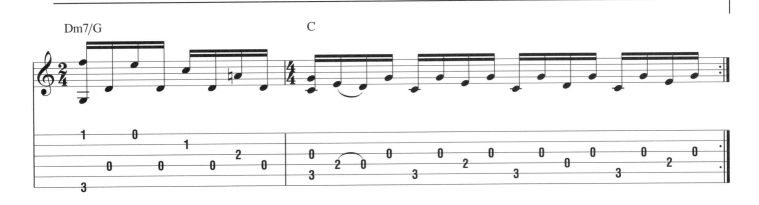

The Godfather
(Love Theme)

from the Paramount Picture THE GODFATHER
By Nino Rota

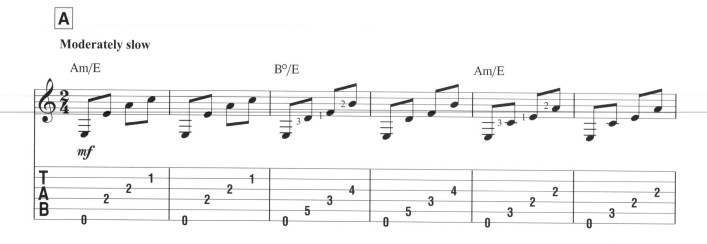

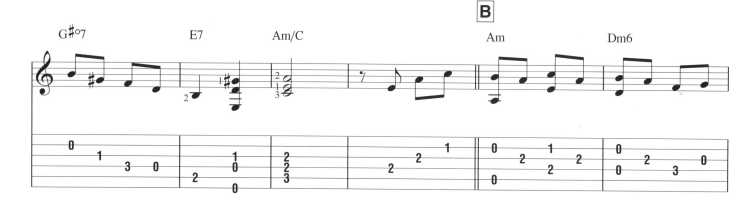

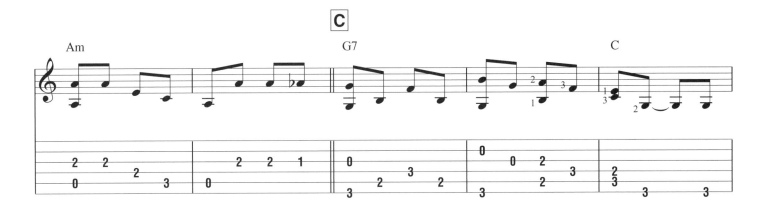

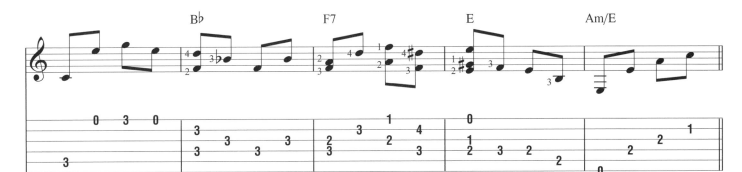

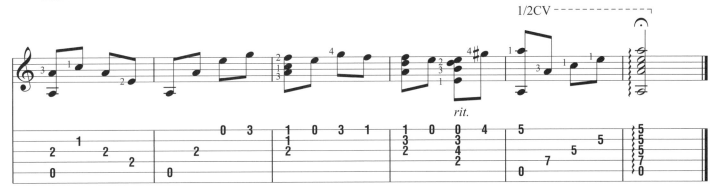

Come Back to Sorrento

By Ernesto de Curtis

Once a - gain to let you hear me tell you of my love so true.

Verse

3. As I wake, my tears are start - ing, think - ing of the hour of part - ing.

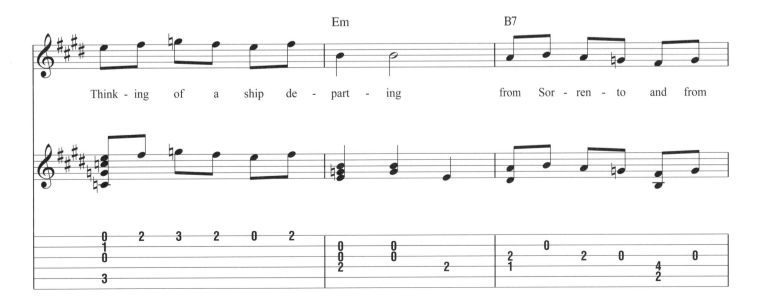

Think - ing of a ship de - part - ing from Sor - ren - to and from

Outro

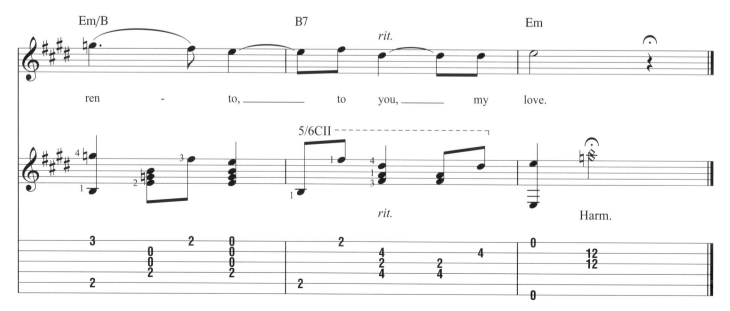

Mambo Italiano

Words and Music by Bob Merrill

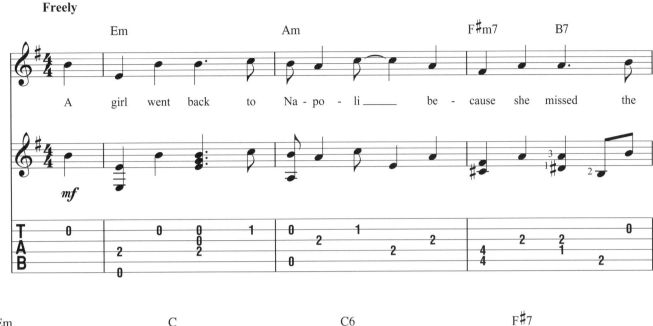

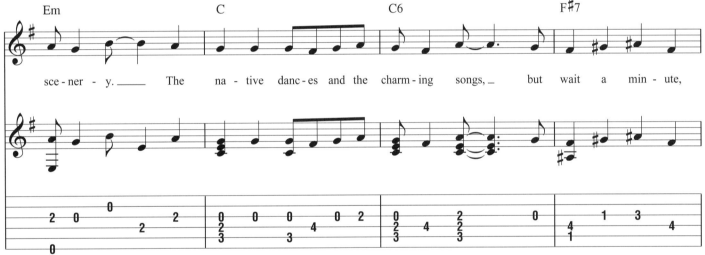

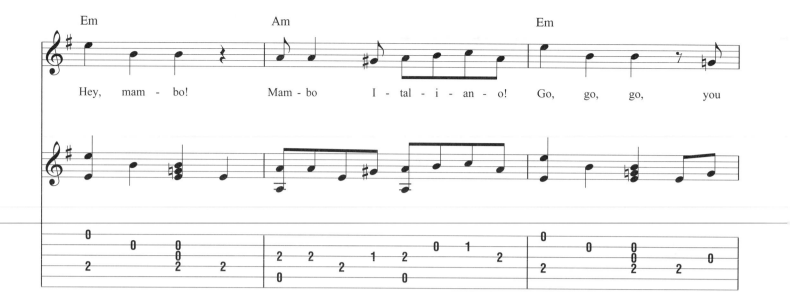

Hey, mam - bo! Mam - bo I - tal - i - an - o! Go, go, go, you

mixed up Si - cil - i - an - o. All you Cal - a - braise - a do the mam - bo like a cra - zy with a

hey, mam - bo! Don't wan - na tar - an - tel - la. Hey, mam - bo!

Bridge

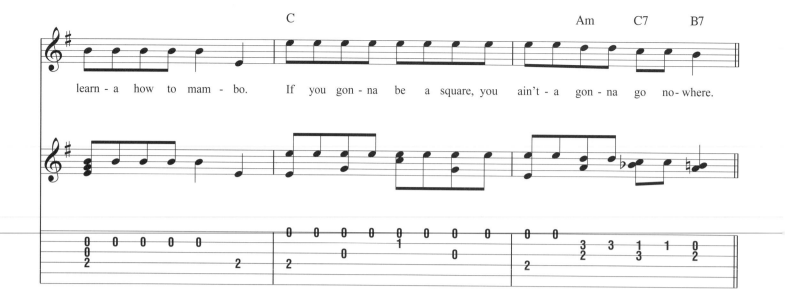

learn - a how to mam - bo. If you gon - na be a square, you ain't - a gon - na go no - where.

Verse

2. Hey, mam - bo! Hey, mam - bo I - tal - i - an - o! Hey, mam - bo! Mam - bo I - tal - i - an - o!
4. *See additional lyrics*

Go, go, Joe. Shake like - a Gi - o - vian - o. Hel - lo, kess - e - deetch, you get - ta

hap - py in the feets a - when you mam - bo _____ I - tal - i -

an - o. _____

an - o. _____

Additional Lyrics

3. Hey, mambo! Hey, mambo Italiano!
   Hey, mambo! Hey, mambo Italiano!
   Bang bongo and throw out the piccolino.
   Shake-a, baby, shake-a 'cause I love-a when you take-a me to

   Hey, mambo! Down by the pizzaria.
   Ho, ho, ho, that's where I'm gonna be-a.
   No, no, no, don't tell-a mama mia.
   Mama say, "You stop-a or I'm gonna tell-a papa," and-a

Bridge: Hey, jadrool, you don't-a have to
   Go to school; just make a
   Beat, bambino; it's-a like a vino.
   Kid, you good-a lookin' but you don't know what's a-cookin' till you

4. Hey, mambo! Hey, mambo Italiano!
   Hey, mambo! Hey, mambo Italiano!
   Ho, ho, ho, you mixed up Siciliano.
   It's-a so delish-a ev'rybody come copish-a how to mambo Italiano.

A Man Without Love
(Quando m'innamoro)

English Lyric by Barry Mason
Original Words and Music by D. Pace, M. Panzeri and R. Livraghi

Verse
Moderately

1. I can re-mem-ber when ____ we walked to-geth-er,

shar-ing a love I thought ____ would last for-ev-er.

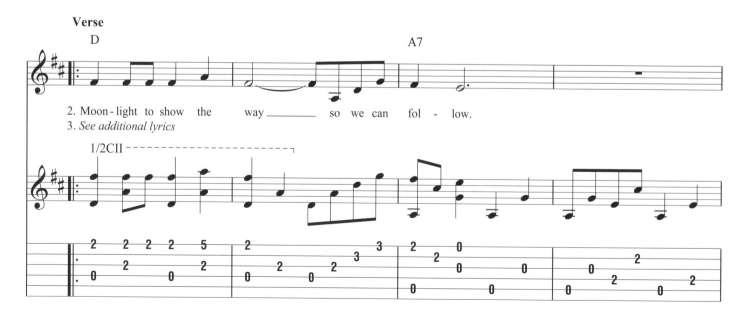

Verse

2. Moon-light to show the way ____ so we can fol-low.
3. *See additional lyrics*

Wait - ing in - side her eyes _____ was my to - mor - row.

Then some - thing changed her mind _____ her kiss - es told me.

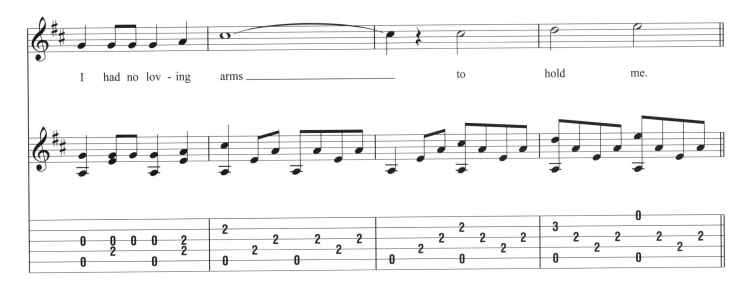

I had no lov - ing arms _____ to hold me.

Additional Lyrics

3. I cannot face this world that's fallen down on me.
So, if you see my girl please send her home to me.
Tell her about my heart that's slowly dying.
Say I can't stop myself from crying.

More
(Ti guarderò nel cuore)

from the film MONDO CANE
Music by Nino Oliviero and Riz Ortolani
Italian Lyrics by Marcello Ciorciolini
English Lyrics by Norman Newell

hold you so; my life will be in your keep - ing, wak - ing, sleep - ing,

Verse

laugh - ing, weep - ing. 2., 4. Long - er than al - ways is a long, long

time; but far be - yond for - ev - er you'll be

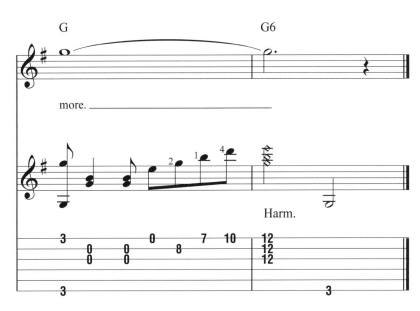

Non Dimenticar
(T'ho voluto bene)
from the Film ANNA

English Lyric by Shelley Dobbins
Original Italian Lyrics by Michele Galdieri
Music by P.G. Redi

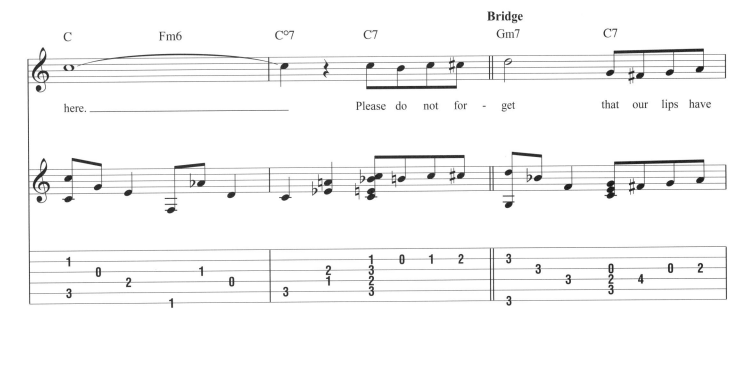

Verse

3. Non di - men - ti - car ___ al - though you trav - el far, ___ my

dar - ling. _____ It's my heart you own so I'll wait a -

lone non di - men - ti - car. _____

Additional Lyrics

2. Non dimenticar my love is like a star, my darling.
   Shining bright and clear just because you're here.

34

Return to Me

Words and Music by Danny Di Minno and Carmen Lombardo

Hur - ry home, hur - ry home. Won't you please hur - ry home to my heart? _____

My dar - ling, if I hurt you, I'm sor - ry. _____

For - give me and please say you are mine. _____

36

Verse

2. Return to me.
4. See additional lyrics

Please come back, bel - la mi - a.

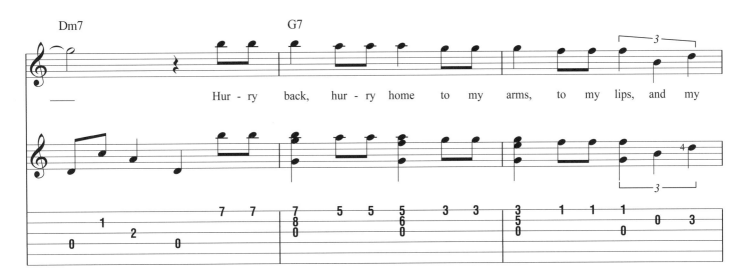

Hur - ry back, hur - ry home to my arms, to my lips, and my

heart.
3. Ri - tor - na a mor!

Additional Lyrics

3. Ritorna a me, non la sciare mi solo.
   Vieni tu, vieni tu, viene tu, viene tu, mi amor.
   Ritorna a me, cara mea ti amo.
   Solo tu, solo tu, solo tu, solo tu, mio cuor.

Bridge: Bambina, dar il couranes suno.
   Mantiene, solamente per me.

4. Ritorna a me, e lasanta venuta.
   Vieni tu, vieni tu, solo tu, solo tu, mi amor!

That's Amore
(That's Love)
from the Paramount Picture THE CADDY

Words by Jack Brooks
Music by Harry Warren

Drop D tuning:
(low to high) D-A-D-G-B-E

Verse
Moderately

1. When the moon hits your eye like a big piz-za pie, that's a-more.
   stars make you drool just like pas-ta fa-zool, that's a-more.

mo-ré. When the world seems to shine like you've
mo-ré. When you dance down the street with a

To Coda

had too much wine, that's a-mo-ré.   Bells will
cloud at your

ring, ting - a - ling - a - ling, ting - a - ling - a - ling, and you'll sing, "Vi - ta bel - la." _____

_____ Hearts will play, tip - py - tip - py - tay, tip - py - tip - py -

D.S. al Coda

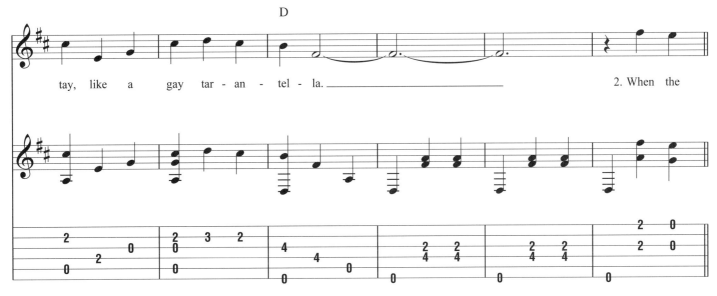

tay, like a gay tar - an - tel - la. _____ 2. When the

⊕ Coda

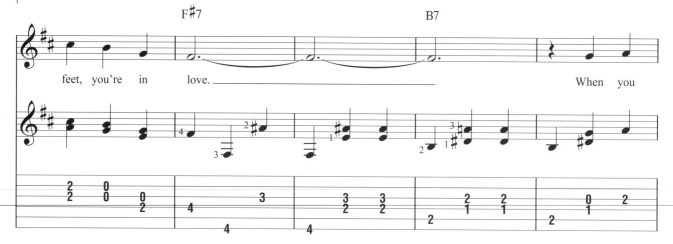

feet, you're in love. _____ When you

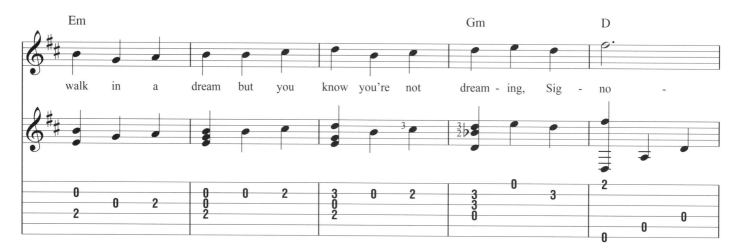

walk in a dream but you know you're not dream-ing, Sig-no-

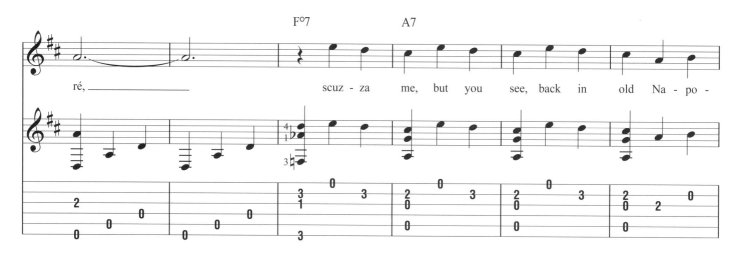

ré, _____ scuz-za me, but you see, back in old Na-po-

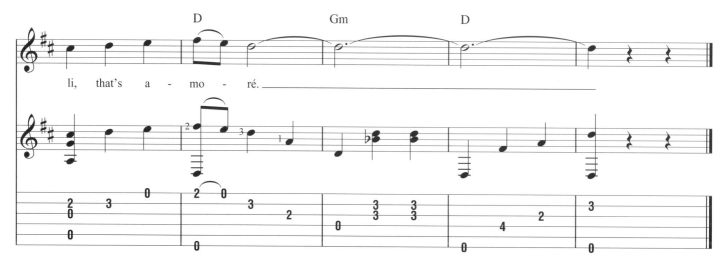

li, that's a-mo-ré. _____

There's No Tomorrow

Written by Al Hoffman, Leo Corday and Leon Carr

let's take that mo - ment that to - night is grant - ing. _____

Chorus

_____ There's no to - mor - row _____ when love is new.

_____ Now is for - ev - er _____ when love is true. _____

So kiss me   and hold   me

tight.   There's no to - mor - row;   there's just to -

night.   There's no to - night.

A Time for Us
(Love Theme)

from the Paramount Picture ROMEO AND JULIET

Words by Larry Kusik and Eddie Snyder
Music by Nino Rota

Chorus

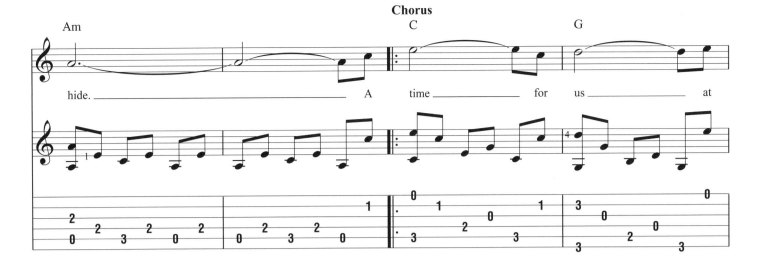

hide._____ A time_____ for us_____ at

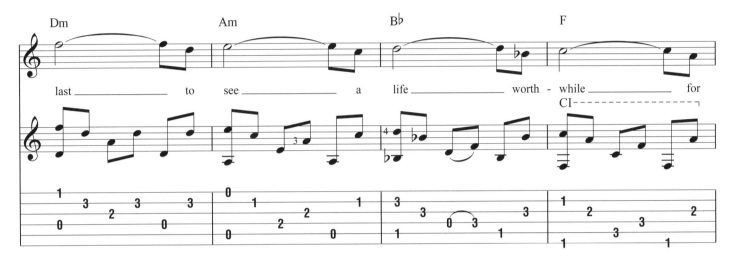

last_____ to see_____ a life_____ worth - while_____ for

Verse

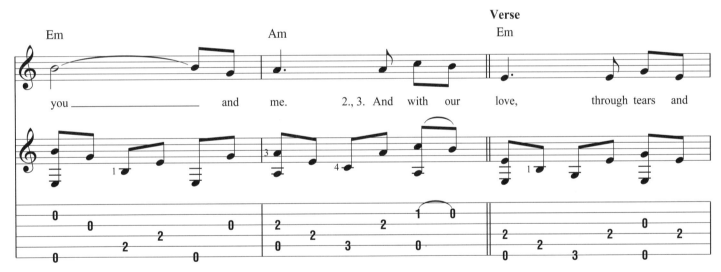

you_____ and me. 2., 3. And with our love, through tears and

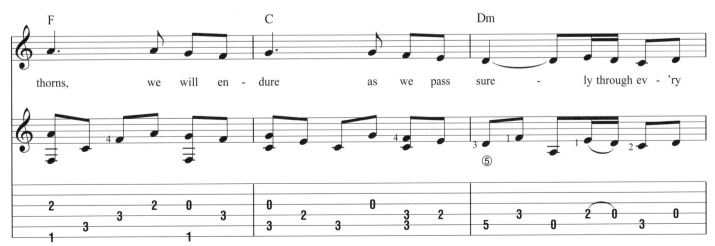

thorns, we will en - dure as we pass sure - ly through ev - 'ry

Volare

Music by Domenico Modugno
English Lyric by Mitchell Parish
Original Italian Text by Domenico Modugno and Francesco Migliacci

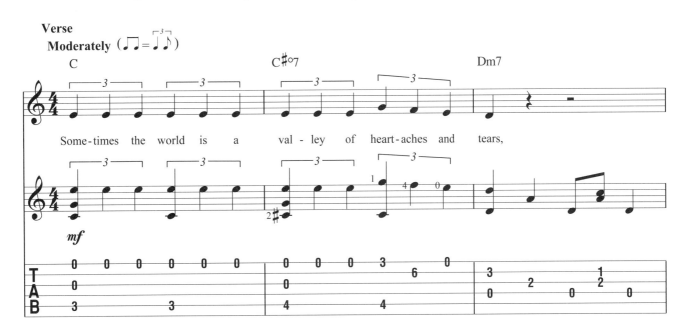

Some-times the world is a val-ley of heart-aches and tears,

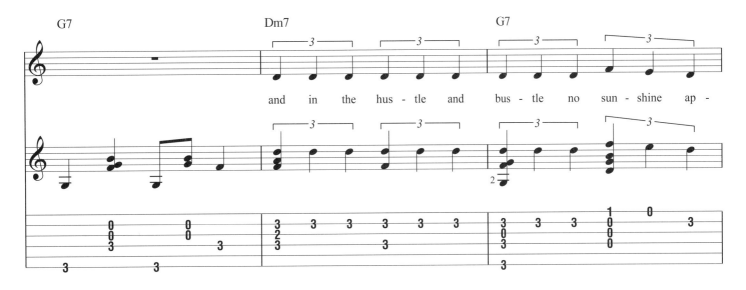

and in the hus-tle and bus-tle no sun-shine ap-

pears.

But you and I have our love al-ways there to re-

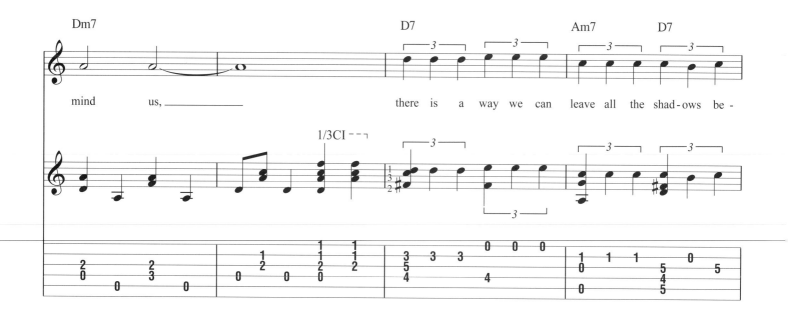

mind us,_____ there is a way we can leave all the shad-ows be-

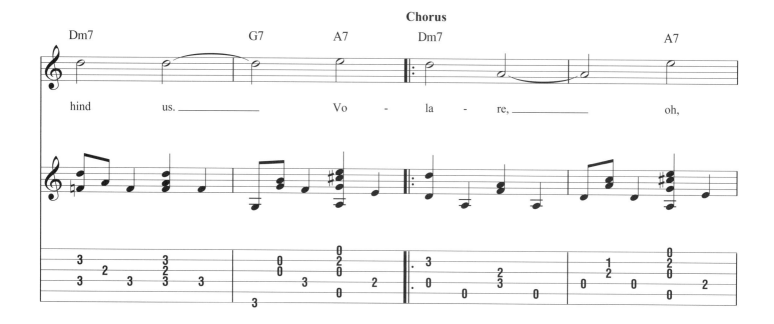

Chorus

hind us._____ Vo - la - re,_____ oh,

oh!_____ Can - ta - re,_____ oh, oh, oh,

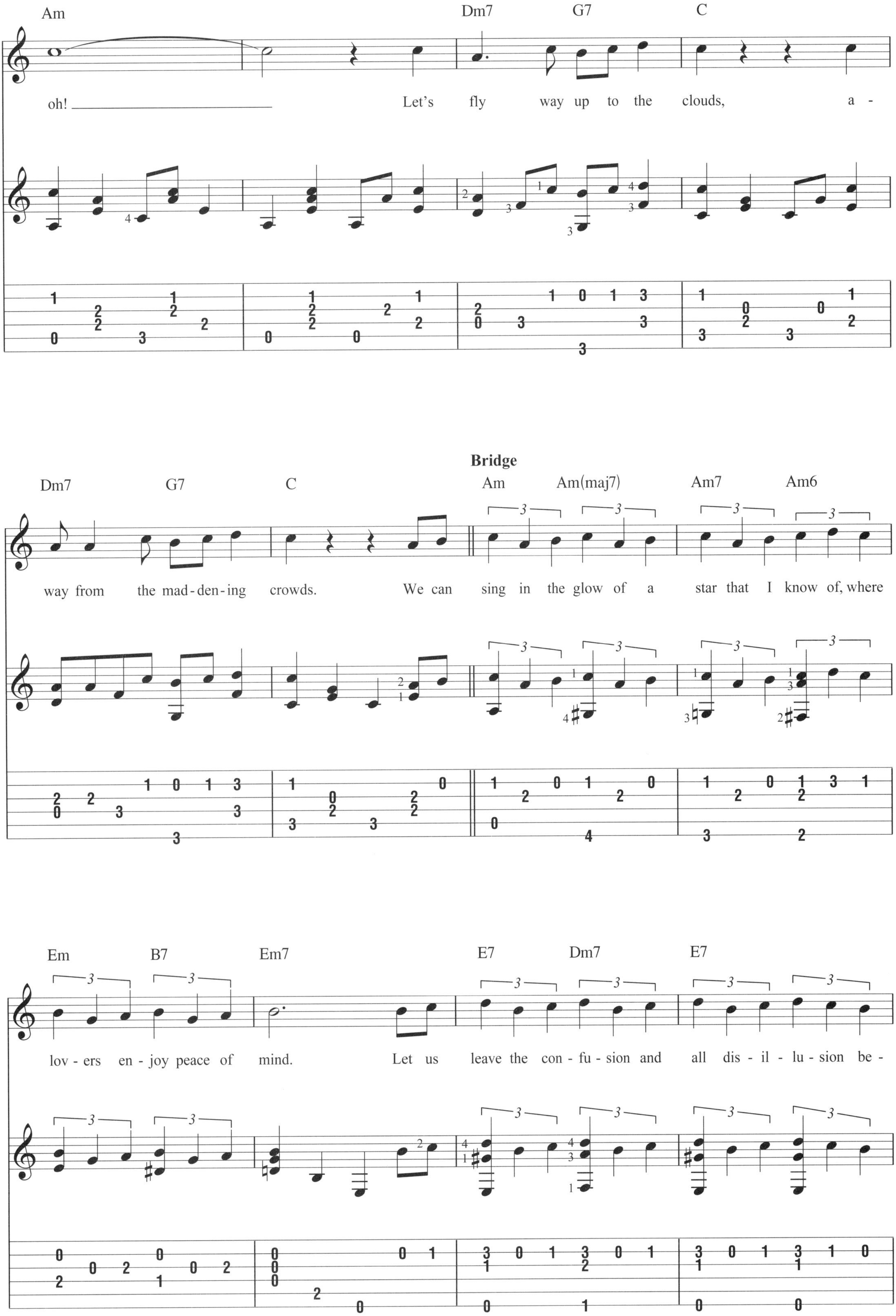
Am
Dm7 G7 C
oh! Let's fly way up to the clouds, a -
Dm7 G7 C
Bridge
Am Am(maj7) Am7 Am6
way from the mad-den-ing crowds. We can sing in the glow of a star that I know of, where
Em B7 Em7 E7 Dm7 E7
lov - ers en - joy peace of mind. Let us leave the con - fu - sion and all dis - il - lu - sion be -

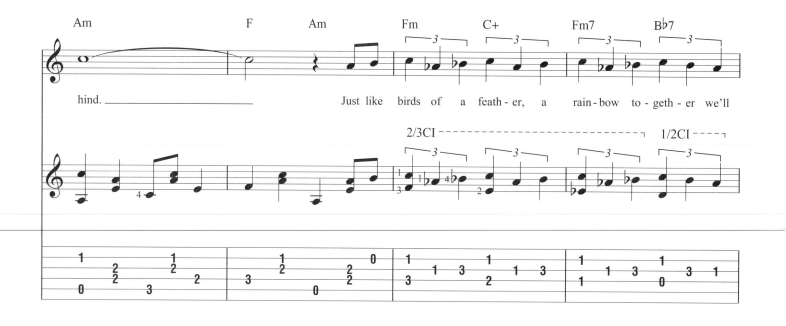

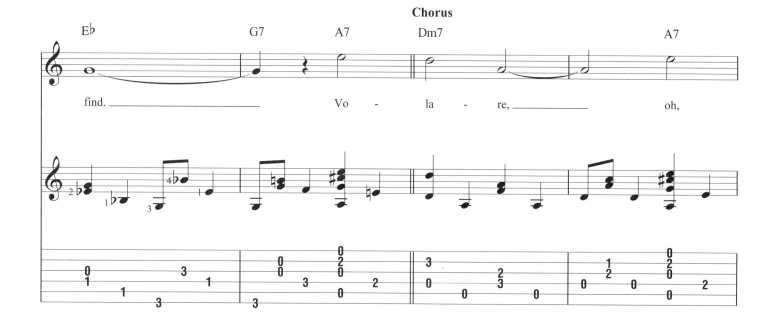

oh! _____ No won-der my hap-py heart sings, your

love has giv-en me wings. Vo - wings. Your

love has giv-en me wings. Your love has giv-en me wings.

You're Breaking My Heart

Words and Music by Pat Genaro and Sunny Skylar

Chorus

joy _____ though tear-drops burn. _____ But if some-day you should want to re-

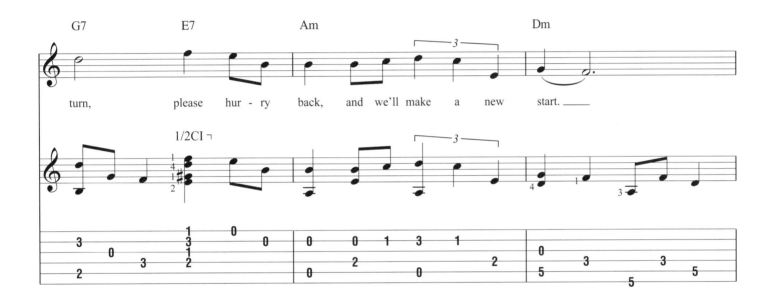

turn, please hur-ry back, and we'll make a new start. _____

'Til then, you're break-ing my heart. _____

Additional Lyrics

2. It's breaking my heart to remember the dreams we depended upon.
   You're leaving is a slow-dying ember; I'll miss you, my love, when you're gone.

FINGERPICKING GUITAR BOOKS

Hone your fingerpicking skills with these great songbooks featuring solo guitar arrangements in standard notation and tablature. The arrangements in these books are carefully written for intermediate-level guitarists. Each song combines melody and harmony in one superb guitar fingerpicking arrangement. Each book also includes an introduction to basic fingerstyle guitar.

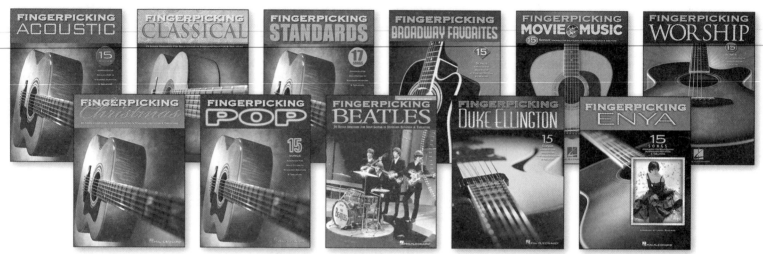

FINGERPICKING ACOUSTIC
00699614.................................$12.99

FINGERPICKING ACOUSTIC CLASSICS
00160211.................................$12.99

FINGERPICKING ACOUSTIC HITS
00160202.................................$12.99

FINGERPICKING ACOUSTIC ROCK
00699764.................................$12.99

FINGERPICKING BACH
00699793.................................$10.99

FINGERPICKING BALLADS
00699717.................................$10.99

FINGERPICKING BEATLES
00699049.................................$19.99

FINGERPICKING BEETHOVEN
00702390...................................$7.99

FINGERPICKING BLUES
00701277 ....$9.99

FINGERPICKING BROADWAY FAVORITES
00699843...................................$9.99

FINGERPICKING BROADWAY HITS
00699838...................................$7.99

FINGERPICKING CELTIC FOLK
00701148.................................$10.99

FINGERPICKING CHILDREN'S SONGS
00699712...................................$9.99

FINGERPICKING CHRISTIAN
00701076 ....$7.99

FINGERPICKING CHRISTMAS
00699599...................................$9.99

FINGERPICKING CHRISTMAS CLASSICS
00701695...................................$7.99

FINGERPICKING CHRISTMAS SONGS
00171333...................................$9.99

FINGERPICKING CLASSICAL
00699620.................................$10.99

FINGERPICKING COUNTRY
00699687.................................$10.99

FINGERPICKING DISNEY
00699711.................................$14.99

FINGERPICKING DUKE ELLINGTON
00699845...................................$9.99

FINGERPICKING ENYA
00701161...................................$9.99

FINGERPICKING FILM SCORE MUSIC
00160143.................................$12.99

FINGERPICKING GOSPEL
00701059...................................$9.99

FINGERPICKING GUITAR BIBLE
00691040 ....$19.99

FINGERPICKING HIT SONGS
00160195.................................$12.99

FINGERPICKING HYMNS
00699688...................................$9.99

FINGERPICKING IRISH SONGS
00701965...................................$9.99

FINGERPICKING JAZZ FAVORITES
00699844...................................$7.99

FINGERPICKING JAZZ STANDARDS
00699840.................................$10.99

FINGERPICKING LATIN FAVORITES
00699842...................................$9.99

FINGERPICKING LATIN STANDARDS
00699837.................................$12.99

FINGERPICKING ANDREW LLOYD WEBBER
00699839.................................$12.99

FINGERPICKING LOVE SONGS
00699841.................................$12.99

FINGERPICKING LOVE STANDARDS
00699836 ....$9.99

FINGERPICKING LULLABYES
00701276.................................$9.99

FINGERPICKING MOVIE MUSIC
00699919.................................$10.99

FINGERPICKING MOZART
00699794...................................$9.99

FINGERPICKING POP
00699615.................................$12.99

FINGERPICKING POPULAR HITS
00139079.................................$12.99

FINGERPICKING PRAISE
00699714...................................$9.99

FINGERPICKING ROCK
00699716.................................$10.99

FINGERPICKING STANDARDS
00699613.................................$12.99

FINGERPICKING WEDDING
00699637...................................$9.99

FINGERPICKING WORSHIP
00700554...................................$9.99

FINGERPICKING NEIL YOUNG – GREATEST HITS
00700134.................................$14.99

FINGERPICKING YULETIDE
00699654...................................$9.99

HAL•LEONARD®

Visit Hal Leonard online at **www.halleonard.com**

Prices, contents and availability
subject to change without notice.

AUTHENTIC CHORDS • ORIGINAL KEYS • COMPLETE SONGS

The *Strum It* series lets players strum the chords and sing along with their favorite hits. Each song has been selected because it can be played with regular open chords, barre chords, or other moveable chord types. Guitarists can simply play the rhythm, or play and sing along through the entire song. All songs are shown in their original keys complete with chords, strum patterns, melody and lyrics. Wherever possible, the chord voicings from the recorded versions are notated.

THE BEACH BOYS' GREATEST HITS
00699357.. $12.95

THE BEATLES FAVORITES
00699249..$15.99

VERY BEST OF JOHNNY CASH
00699514..$14.99

CELTIC GUITAR SONGBOOK
00699265..$9.95

CHRISTMAS SONGS FOR GUITAR
00699247..$10.95

CHRISTMAS SONGS WITH 3 CHORDS
00699487..$9.99

VERY BEST OF ERIC CLAPTON
00699560..$12.95

JIM CROCE – CLASSIC HITS
00699269..$10.95

DISNEY FAVORITES
00699171..$12.99

MELISSA ETHERIDGE GREATEST HITS
00699518..$12.99

FAVORITE SONGS WITH 3 CHORDS
00699112..$10.99

FAVORITE SONGS WITH 4 CHORDS
00699270..$8.95

FIRESIDE SING-ALONG
00699273..$10.99

FOLK FAVORITES
00699517..$8.95

THE GUITAR STRUMMERS' ROCK SONGBOOK
00701678..$14.99

BEST OF WOODY GUTHRIE
00699496..$12.95

JOHN HIATT COLLECTION
00699398..$16.99

THE VERY BEST OF BOB MARLEY
00699524..$14.99

A MERRY CHRISTMAS SONGBOOK
00699211..$9.95

MORE FAVORITE SONGS WITH 3 CHORDS
00699532..$9.99

THE VERY BEST OF TOM PETTY
00699336..$14.99

ELVIS! GREATEST HITS
00699276..$10.95

BEST OF GEORGE STRAIT
00699235..$16.99

TAYLOR SWIFT FOR ACOUSTIC GUITAR
00109717..$16.99

BEST OF HANK WILLIAMS JR.
00699224..$15.99

Prices, contents & availability
subject to change without notice.

HAL•LEONARD®

Visit Hal Leonard online at
www.halleonard.com

0318

JAZZ GUITAR CHORD MELODY SOLOS

This series features chord melody arrangements in standard notation and tablature of songs for intermediate guitarists. **INCLUDES TAB**

ALL-TIME STANDARDS

27 songs, including: All of Me • Bewitched • Come Fly with Me • A Fine Romance • Georgia on My Mind • How High the Moon • I'll Never Smile Again • I've Got You Under My Skin • It's De-Lovely • It's Only a Paper Moon • My Romance • Satin Doll • The Surrey with the Fringe on Top • Yesterdays • and more.
00699757 Solo Guitar....................$14.99

IRVING BERLIN

27 songs, including: Alexander's Ragtime Band • Always • Blue Skies • Cheek to Cheek • Easter Parade • Happy Holiday • Heat Wave • How Deep Is the Ocean • Puttin' On the Ritz • Remember • They Say It's Wonderful • What'll I Do? • White Christmas • and more.
00700637 Solo Guitar....................$14.99

CHRISTMAS CAROLS

26 songs, including: Auld Lang Syne • Away in a Manger • Deck the Hall • God Rest Ye Merry, Gentlemen • Good King Wenceslas • Here We Come A-Wassailing • It Came upon the Midnight Clear • Joy to the World • O Holy Night • O Little Town of Bethlehem • Silent Night • Toyland • We Three Kings of Orient Are • and more.
00701697 Solo Guitar....................$12.99

CHRISTMAS JAZZ

21 songs, including Auld Lang Syne • Baby, It's Cold Outside • Cool Yule • Have Yourself a Merry Little Christmas • I've Got My Love to Keep Me Warm • Mary, Did You Know? • Santa Baby • Sleigh Ride • White Christmas • Winter Wonderland • and more.
00171334 Solo Guitar....................$14.99

DISNEY SONGS

27 songs, including: Beauty and the Beast • Can You Feel the Love Tonight • Candle on the Water • Colors of the Wind • A Dream Is a Wish Your Heart Makes • Heigh-Ho • Some Day My Prince Will Come • Under the Sea • When You Wish upon a Star • A Whole New World (Aladdin's Theme) • Zip-A-Dee-Doo-Dah • and more.
00701902 Solo Guitar....................$14.99

DUKE ELLINGTON

25 songs, including: C-Jam Blues • Caravan • Do Nothin' Till You Hear from Me • Don't Get Around Much Anymore • I Got It Bad and That Ain't Good • I'm Just a Lucky So and So • In a Sentimental Mood • It Don't Mean a Thing (If It Ain't Got That Swing) • Mood Indigo • Perdido • Prelude to a Kiss • Satin Doll • and more.
00700636 Solo Guitar....................$12.99

FAVORITE STANDARDS

27 songs, including: All the Way • Autumn in New York • Blue Skies • Cheek to Cheek • Don't Get Around Much Anymore • How Deep Is the Ocean • I'll Be Seeing You • Isn't It Romantic? • It Could Happen to You • The Lady Is a Tramp • Moon River • Speak Low • Take the "A" Train • Willow Weep for Me • Witchcraft • and more.
00699756 Solo Guitar....................$14.99

JAZZ BALLADS

27 songs, including: Body and Soul • Darn That Dream • Easy to Love (You'd Be So Easy to Love) • Here's That Rainy Day • In a Sentimental Mood • Misty • My Foolish Heart • My Funny Valentine • The Nearness of You • Stella by Starlight • Time After Time • The Way You Look Tonight • When Sunny Gets Blue • and more.
00699755 Solo Guitar....................$14.99

LATIN STANDARDS

27 Latin favorites, including: Água De Beber (Water to Drink) • Desafinado • The Girl from Ipanema • How Insensitive (Insensatez) • Little Boat • Meditation • One Note Samba (Samba De Uma Nota So) • Poinciana • Quiet Nights of Quiet Stars • Samba De Orfeu • So Nice (Summer Samba) • Wave • and more.
00699754 Solo Guitar....................$14.99

HAL•LEONARD®

www.halleonard.com